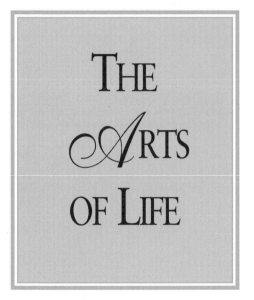

THE ARTS OF LIFE

A collection of thoughts by Anthea Church on the deeper meaning of life's arts and positive attributes which can be acquired through the positive thinking and Raja Yoga meditation techniques taught by the Brahma Kumaris World Spiritual University

ARTS OF LIFE

First Edition 1989

Second Edition January 1990

Third Edition January 1995

ISBN 0-9637396-2-X

Published by the Brahma Kumaris World Spiritual University,
Literature Department, 65 Pound Lane, London NW10 2HH UK

There are Brahma Kumaris Centres in over 62 countries worldwide.

Printed by Waterside Litho, Chesham UK

Available in other languages

*This book has beeen compiled and edited by the Brahma Kumaris World Spiritual
University, a non-profit organisation, with the aim of sharing information as a
community service for the spiritual growth of individuals.*

C ONTENTS

FOREWORD

The greatest art is to be silent. Not just unspeaking with the lips, but unspeaking with the mind. When the mind is quiet, its whole angle of vision changes. From pouncing on the problems, it begins to perceive the chances, the good things in life; and, in that discrimination which comes from silence, lie all other arts. The arts that make life a pleasure and a challenge; like how to talk to each other, entertain each other, accept each other - in short, how to be happy not just together, but alone.

For alone is where it all begins. We come alone and we go alone. And though we can learn a lot from each other, the things that are most valuable and apart completely from the rough and tumble of life are conceived quietly. It is these that are the seeds of our future as opposed to the patching up of our past.

Anthea Church

THE
*A*RT OF
ADMINISTRATION

If you are a good administrator, you are known by everyone and yet you only know yourself. So deeply though that the harmony inside shines out, in a way it wouldn't if you looked outwards first and then studied. An art cannot be learnt from looking out. It is a gift that comes from looking in - at yourself.

You live in a body and that has to be known, not physiologically, as a machine, but spiritually, as a temple. When you know it physiologically, you cure it with chemicals; when you know it spiritually, you cure it with thought. And when its health is based on thought, it becomes a source of health to others - a refuge. When it's health is based on medicine, it becomes an attraction to others and so a trap.

And who are you that lives there? You are a thinker, and what you think makes the atmosphere in the 'temple', and the atmosphere determines how much love there is in your life. A poor thinker in a smart machine attracts friendship with a motive; a rich thinker in a temple attracts love. And the love that you attract today is the foundation of your future, so though it is earned slowly, it's depth is worth it.

And when your thinking is unusual and far-reaching, your body becomes the same. Arms move easily; people say 'yes' when logic says no. And the body ceases to be a machine which needs fixed things - it becomes alive as you are, for deep thought penetrates and changes even matter. To the point where consciously, you can invest virtue in your limbs and the work that they do, up to now a chore, will reach out and touch people. This is good administration, for then your heart isn't just pumping oxygen to the organs, it is drawing people together; your brain not just sending messages to your limbs, but to other people. This is real change. When work has become spiritual and big.

Just doing a task is labour. Expressing a quality through it is wealth. And in the future, it won't be a case of different levels any more; of matching fact and inspiration, physical and spiritual. For the spirit will still be separate but it will flow into the physical, which itself will be strong enough to receive and express it - as though spontaneously, but yet in balance. And balance knows that too much of anything, however beautiful, makes sickness.

Administrator is a cold word. No touching. In the future there will be warmth and intimacy in it that take 'ruling' right out of the language. For all will bring to life what is special in them and that, however small, will be invaluable. You may stand still and watch your wishes expressed, but they will be the wishes felt by everyone, and there will be' no more need for negotiation than there would need be between the mind and the heart. The heart pumps because that is its nature. The body of the kingdom will be the same.

And there will be such a force towards equality too; such a caring that if someone were to feel an intensity of emotion, however merited - even as they stand and watch the birth of their child - they would give that over to you, and as administrator, you'd send it to a flagging limb somewhere. For even now, in your body, a sudden pang of feeling is unbalancing and makes you move unevenly and stumble when it has gone. To administrate is to keep nothing, but to put all things where they're needed.

That is the future. Now you have only yourself to care for and you will see that inside is a being tipped towards the past and so outside is a body erratic and unpredictable. To administrate now means never to hate. Always to stay level-headed, even when the past like a jester comes and kicks your thinking; and in the calmness, memory jumps in.

It is very personal. It has only to do with you, and yet the more careful you are with life, the more public you become; and then determination pulls a task towards you, love sets it in motion, peace carries it through. An administrator of the future is a person for whom now, there is introversion but no privacy; for whom every thought draws a thousand hands to make it practical; for whom there are no secrets, because God has opened the doors and told the world they can come in.

The
Art of
Communication

The crux of communication is wastage. In writing, the search for expression, the sensitivity to its reception, the pressure of time, drain away the energy of thought at its conception. When it arrives on paper, it is diluted (or exaggerated); when it arrives in the reader's hands, it is three days late and he/she is busy. "Might" is read for "won't"; "sorry" for "can't"; "love" for "much love" and meanwhile the writer is somewhere else. In speech, instead of doing, doing is spoken of, and the gap between the two takes action away until instead of loving a person, you call them "love" and that makes up for it. But "love" means "leave me alone"; "thanks" means "hurry up"; silence means "I'm tired " or "busy". Moments when speech meets action; and both spring out of a single thought into clear expression, are as rare as elm trees. And everything slips and changes so that elm trees and rarity only make sense in England in the eighties. Yesterday, tomorrow, somewhere else, the analogy is useless.

There are moments when eyes catch eyes and the pressure of this, the contact, far closer than any touch, deflects dignity into an expression of awkward sincerity and though words don't say it, hesitation does and arms and legs stutter your meaning. These moments are breaking points, but they hurt, for the shame of nudity, unforeseen, is difficult. You need time to get the machine running smoothly again.

There are gaps in the darkness; semi-openness, semi-honesty. Funny people convey truth in their humour and serious people seek out quality in their friendships, and sometimes life produces a collision which breaks everything up and value shines through.

It won't always just be a glimmer.

A day will come when what you think, do and say, will all be equal expressions of one force. And the force will be you. Not a mixture of conscience and impulse, duty and desire. Just you. You will just live. And what you are living will be part of the river that will run through everyone. The landscape of your mind will be unique, but the water will be the same and it will be clean.

What will words be then? Words will explain things that would take too long to show, like how to climb a mountain. Words will represent things. But they won't convey feeling, for the body will do that. The deepest through the eyes, the lightest through the arms....The body will speak. And so will the air, for with the change of a thought, its texture will change and be felt. And words will be destinations, not journeys. They will not express hope or intention. They will be like palaces as opposed to tents. There would be no point decorating a tent, because it is always being moved. But a palace is fixed, traditional, rich. So too words. There will be no irony, no sarcasm, no ambiguity, for these destroy value. Instead words will be filled with depth, age, and above all resonance, because they will be "places" of meeting and enjoyment, free of the ego of debate or discussion.

It won't be boring, for the senses will provide stimulation. Where words are fixed, they can be enhanced. A word may be as fragrant as a garden, and so a good conversation will be as refreshing as a walk, and it probably would be held whilst walking anyway, for what is inside you will be married to what you see. And as you speak to someone, an image will be projected on to their mind's eye and as you converse, you will both add to it like painters standing before one canvas. Creativity will be your meeting point.

Life will be quieter. The air will be less disturbed, more spacious. For words are as cumbersome as objects, so that you can walk into an unfurnished room where there has been an argument and it will seem full.

And what of communicating at a distance? That will be the task of the brain. For where your brain sends messages to your body now, it will do the same then, but to any body, not only to your own. The message will be registered on someone else's brain simply and clearly and then the soul, watching, apart and self-knowing, will reply. And where love is very deep and pure, it will by-pass the systems and formality of the brain, and soul will meet soul in silent union, like two springs underground, joining.

You cannot learn to communicate like that from a human being. For a human is filled with the past and every word spoken is weighted by that. Love felt deeply has desire in it somewhere. You have to learn it from God. It is called yoga.

God can put everything into a nothing and he will make your everything an irrelevance. He wouldn't touch your philosophy, but he could teach you everything on a thumbnail, if that's all there was. So he makes you a child again which is beautiful, because to find the future, you have to have a taste for what the world will call idiocy, but time will call a divine joke.

THE
ART OF
DEALING WITH OTHERS

'Dealing' with another human being is like acknowledging a house filled with the possessions, the atmosphere, the colours of a lifetime. In every corner the imprint of an experience. Every room has opened its doors to tens, hundreds, if not people, then at least thoughts. Then single minded and innocent, you walk into that room in search of a possession you have already pictured. You walk into the house, into the room, over to the place where it stands and you take it, to house in your own home. And as you begin to hold that possession close, cherish it and use it, you think you have the whole house in hand, when you know nothing more than you would by holding in your hands a hair from their head.

You feel that you know them perhaps because you chose them for this 'hair', this ornament of their personality and this is why it is so upsetting, so much of an affront, when one day the picture is broken. One day, entering their house, drawn by the prospect of discovering more beauty you can take, you see the house untidy and you are thrown, because before they were just a decoration and they fitted, and now you find their being is a household, even bigger than your own. And it cannot be dismissed as ugly, because amongst the clutter, there are treasures that are beautiful. So then you try to house this new unwielding image in your mind but it is hard, because it has so many patterns, such a past, multi-coloured, and you only know how to respond to blues and greens. So you break the image and walk out.

Dealing with others takes a big heart. To accommodate and enjoy their whole world in all its complexity and not demand that you'll ever totally understand. To assume nothing. Who knows what you may find in a cupboard one day! It means letting all the clutter of a person's past, and your own, rise to the surface and quietly be moulded into use or just die, with no recriminations. For when the muscles are relaxed, when there is no tautness, hurdles are cleared. And not fast, but with grace and richness. Forceful, tensed success shuts part of people out because time demands it, or public image, and then one day, what is pushed away bursts out and breaks all that has been made, like a sleeptalker revealing fear.

Dealing with others is equanimity in the face of what you like and what you don't, knowing that whilst a branch is twisted and awkward, a tree has dignity, as all beings do, in their entirety.

It is recognising that everything is in the design. To number a human being is to imprison them and yet, it is true that everyone is numbered, has a place, is in a sequence. Dealing with others is knowing their number, but not placing a fixed value on it, for even in a game of cards, a six is a trump in one game and the kings and queens are redundant. Everything changes. The context makes the value. Dealing with others is knowing where a number fits according to the game, watching value change. To hold someone at one value is to kill their growth and their beauty.

It is a great openness that is needed, an openness that lets life come and go, in and out, flow, change. So that nothing is lodged, obstructing. Each situation, however identical it seems, is new. It is breaking down reflexes, habits, patterns.

It begins in the mind. To deal with others, there has to be mastery over your mind; a discipline and love that, not needing expression, calls all minds to order, pulling, attracting like a magnet. Not issuing orders, but being ordered.

To issue makes people jump into action, jars nerves, forces. To be ordered beckons them into quietness, makes an inroad into their chatter, so that they listen. This state of mind, calls across space to all minds; it calls to order and silence those present, but also those distant. It can achieve miracles of organisation; it does not need recognition; it is to do with creating, not hurting; it does not jump on anyone's back. It is professionalism.

To deal with others, you have to know who you are, what is your number, what is your role, what is the game. If four is not in place, nor can be five, six, seven, eight.. It is a task for yourself. It is a task for silence. And the more people there are standing in front of you watching, the more public the duty, the more private and free your mind needs to be.

Imagine standing in front of someone and seeing their whole world in front of you, seeing their past, their future, seeing their talents, their nature, not as in a book, sectioned, chaptered, detailed, but in one fell swoop, swiftly, passing, like a kaleidoscope. Now imagine seeing that same person taking the joy out of someone's achievement and realising suddenly they did so because they were feeling miserable. Imagine seeing that one blur of muddied colour, like a scrumpled cushion, and going away just with that.

That is the difference between now and the future.

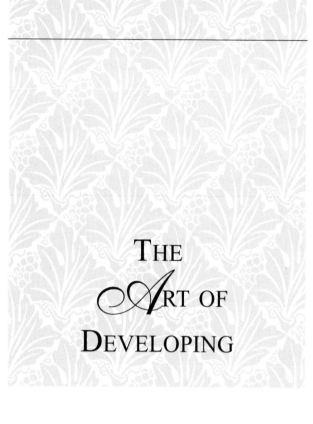

THE
ART OF
DEVELOPING

Developing is the gift of a child, but the art of an adult. It can be worked for, but essentially it is natural; the natural of being unformed, young, soft boned. Taking things as they come, not stiffening out of fear from the past or anticipation of the future. It is expected of children that they do not know that they will grow and change from one moment to the next, but for the adult it is not and this is why it becomes an art. And if not precisely learned it is called instability or fluctuation.

So what is this art? It is to retain for your life a structure that comes to be relied upon. But inside that, it is to be yielding and vigilant. Never to allow toughness to stop growth, but never to allow the pangs of growing to blur the edges of life's visible form.

The art is contrast. The more vulnerable and changing you are, the more you need a task that is fixed. For a task is a shell, but it holds inside it new life. Sometimes when developing there is the impulse to be alone and quiet, but this is exposing yourself to examination. It is like saying: I am alone, ready, look at me; when you are not ready and you are sensitive.

Even to alternate periods of activity with periods of quiet has its shortcomings, for who knows whether the strength of the quiet will meet and nourish the activity or not? It may not help at all. But kept together, that is, action done in quietness, cannot fail to be strong and protective of your inner world. In this strength, development gets its chance; in alternation, it is probably just a case of action followed by recovery.

The art of developing is different from the development of a child. For in it is a vision of what is possible, an aim. It is a long silent journey to a place you have dreamt of and are remembering, though the twists and turns on the way are unforeseen and sudden which is why again, it is best to feel them from inside.

A nd on that journey, to what you know instinctively is what you are, you need balance: between making it happen and just watching it come. To make it happen is in fact not so hard. It is only a matter of obedience - to rules which are unspoken, but when followed, keep you on the main road. For the way has been made before and the road has widened before you, so you only have to walk it. Gently, with faith. If you break the rules, you come to a side road, which however attractive initially, gives no more than a rest, a change. At the point of fatigue, the best thing to do is to proceed, for fatigue is born of fear and fear dies if you go on.

B reaking the rules means giving undue attention to things that life is not obviously presenting you with, like the past, like the future, like friendship not already offered. Such seeking is often called being creative, developing, appreciating newness, but it is moving away from what is there and hidden in what is there, are all the ingredients for what is new. The natural ingredients. To move away from that is having a 'tipple'. It gives eloquence and power, but only for a moment and then you are tired again.

D eveloping is born of simplicity, not grandiose scheming. Just living. Again and again putting one foot in front of the other, eyes ahead, alone, undemanding. The feelings that this brings are deep, long-lasting ones and grow gradually to a point at which you feel an enormity around you.

E normity is when life through action becomes small and structured, but behind each move there's a universe. Life becomes a symbol; the tip of an iceberg. Inside the future is forming.

A nd finally when all is complete within, when all is fully formed and ready, the shell of action breaks and what emerges is a moving living form of pure quality. Quality that can be drawn upon and used, unhampered by time and place. It is just a resource. And it can't be harmed.

I f physical development would be to see a city growing; resources, attractions, population expanding; spiritual developing would be like seeing the whole city melt away until the land stood clear and green and still, awaiting something of a completely new order.

D eveloping needs a new birth.

THE ART OF KEEPING OTHERS CONTENTED AND HAPPY

This is an art for the faithful, for where there is faith, you are just yourself and you just 'do' for the love of it, without seeking anything. It is a way of being, to keep others content, not a decision. If you decide, you are dividing yourself from life and presuming to know. But everyone is a world and no one has wealth enough to travel it completely, to know it. Others need the strangest things sometimes ....

To keep others content though, you have to want to, because you love the collective beauty that contentment brings to life: absorption to a room full of people, balance to a family, mastery to a challenge. You want to because you love the quality and because you love people, but not as a doctor giving an injection, coolly providing health - for that is short-lived. For something to last, you have to live it, be it too, and let it live through you - not offer it on the end of a needle. You give it because you are it completely and it spills over.

To spill over, go deeply inside, not to hide or to recover, but to appreciate yourself. Inside is a still point, a core that touched, breaks open, up to the surface. And when it becomes a spring bubbling out, it is for everyone to drink from, for truth however personal, is never private and always loved. When people say the truth is hard, there is a lie in it somewhere.

You have to go alone to find the core, to take nothing with you. You can't take sadness or you'll get lost on the way;you can't be incomplete or you'll get caught by something that offers itself from outside. It's a journey that costs a lot, as any world tour does - and the money comes from work. To work physically, communally, co-operatively, humbly, minute by minute, earns you a ticket for quiet and leaves the surface untroubled by your departure. There is no hieing off mid-week, when words still need you, when life is calling you. Work, work, then quiet and with practice, work, work and quiet.

Done together, work and quiet, everyone is happy, those for whom what is seen must be completed and those for whom what is unseen must be started. All smile for there is no neglect. And the cushions straightened carefully, with a care found at the core of you, nourish a thousand hearts a way away.

One day, contentment will just be a game. When a man can be womanly, a woman manly, a king can become a child and a child a teacher, when letting go of roles will be as easy as letting someone else have the ball - then contentment will be a game. Sometimes one will make the thought and another's hands will move - easily, happily. Sometimes the second will make the thought and the first will move and neither will be the less for it, for through the thought and the action will run the same unbroken feeling that this is right and needed. And even if the two never see each other, still if the thought of one has met the hands of the other and the task has been accomplished, the same fruit will be shared. And the hands will be beautiful for they will frame the thought in form. This is contentment at its most natural for it is mutual and doesn't need a second's negotiation.

And it is a matter of timing largely. Life has a rhythm somewhere underneath, that heard and heeded, tells you how to pace things. If you feel that you're not keeping people contented, it's probably because you are out of time, wrong only in as much as that. It is subtle, for one beat out can destroy the tune, one thought too much of love can make a head turn when it should face forwards and proceed. But it doesn't, it falters and then there's a tiny flare of anger, then a fire, then, then, then ....

But it's underneath it all that the rhythm plays. It is not to be found in the mind of any single person. To seek it there is to enter an illusion or worse, an unhappy dream, where one thing is completed and something else destroyed. An endless frustration. One person happy, but always at the expense of another. Hear the rhythm of the universe and let life tap that out and everyone starts singing. Some high, some low, some the melody, others the accompaniment and some silent, for music is made by the spaces as well as by the notes.

It is the art then not of keeping others happy and contented, but of being that anyway, in equality. Good games have no leaders.

THE
*A*RT OF
KEEPING SECRETS

When you have left behind the need to think and instead you just do and it is right, this art is yours. When there is one person inside you not two and with the freedom that brings, you can see life for what it is and not for what you want it to be, then you do not even have to choose what to conceal and what to speak of. The choice is made for you by a script that has its own perfection.

When there is a feeling of wholeness inside you, you can see the unbroken line of time that makes the play you're acting in. And when you trust that, you stop deciding on the basis of the present or the past, but you let life unfold in front of you. You trust the script and what it holds and you do not feel the compulsion to create for it makes chaos when all the actors choose the script themselves. Instead you follow and in following, the secrets come.

And the secrets tell of what's to be and when you have seen that, you can relax. But strangely, that's the hardest thing to do, for endeavour is such a habit. It has given you your self-value. But all that is really valuable is inherent, not made. Your value is what has been inside you always, not what you've created. So all you have to do is watch as that is called upon and needed.

The art is in the script, which is so impeccable in what it reveals and what it hides. It knows that something said takes shape and to say it early is as damaging as playing out the last scene first. You may know of what's to come but it has to wait inside you, as a glimpse and even then, you mustn't say it's yours for nothing is; it is in the script and however extraordinary the lines, you are just an actor and you'll go home at the end, ordinary, like everyone else.

The part is given in trust, to be held gently.

Even God is a trustee of his lines, for his part is written too and if the earth were calling out for him, he could not speak and tell you who he is, until the right cue came.

It is hard, but it is also beautiful, because you know that nothing can go wrong. Even if you wished to, you couldn't speak a secret before its time for if you did, no one would hear it. But still, you research and discover in your thinking; and that is your right as an actor - to study and appreciate the ins and outs of what you are playing. But if you hit on something invaluable, watch how there is a diversion away from it - a hubbub that blurs the focus, for value pounced on is destroyed. So the noise that you feel to be carelessness, is in fact your protection and the laughter that takes your intensity, a medicine for nerves that would dance too hard if you robbed them of the soothingness of superficiality.

So thanks are owed to the script for its gift of comedy and love, for the space it gives for you to watch and be at one with people and then to leave the party laughing and to sit and think. For at the most crucial moments the virtue of the play is understatement, for it saves your energy like gold.

And even if you falter; in tiredness to suddenly draw out your savings and blurt out something from the core of you - a secret - instead of going on unbrokenly with life's chores, then that is good too, for in its indignity, it will break your ego and yet open someone else's eyes and the hurt that you feel will in itself be a protection from thinking that you've said something wise, which anyway you haven't because it's simply in the script which isn't yours.

And the script is a perfect liar sometimes, which it has to be to look after something as precious as the future, without hands tampering. And the more you see that, the lies, the more you have to be scrupulous in your honesty, for it's an age of truth that's coming and one step wrong now will be a whole nation's detour later. When the seed opens.

It is a matter of being a child and having trust and yet being careful, quiet, because if you speak to someone tied to you emotionally, the same law applies. They will not hear you properly. They'll think of you only in terms of what you say. Only the script and God coolly know your weakness in its entirety and knowing it, do not cancel out your value. People are confused by paradox but it's at the heart of the play.

To be quiet, but not too much, because that moves people away from you. And little exchanges about potatoes and the news are the small change in your pocket which you need so much until the end. They bring the contrast and keep your heart light, because sometimes things held inside weigh you down and make you crusty and a handful to be with.

As an artist, seek perfection in private - a private that is woven in with the 'potatoes' - for although it is all a play, there should be no performers.

THE
$\mathscr{A}$RT OF
LEADERSHIP

L eadership needs joy. Joy is a force that can penetrate old systems with a new vision. Old systems tend to be material;they become fixed. Only joy can shift them. To lead is to dislodge the old and create the new. And where does joy come from? It comes from the depth of you; it comes from your self-knowledge. Flailing about on the surface produces a web of attitudes that get things done: assertiveness, efficiency, dynamism, but depth produces joy and joy changes things.

L eadership as an art is not to do with being in charge of people, it is to do with command of quality. When there is inside you a flawless quality, something that has been preserved or nurtured - in the instant when that quality is needed, you become a leader. Not you, but it, your love, your charm leads and because it springs from your depths, it projects deep into situations; it reaches the heart and changes it. Quality is the leader.

P roblems only come when people lead, for standing out and above, their whole being projects and whilst their dedication will touch some, their fear will hurt others. Where only quality leads, there is no name, there is no figurehead - there is just a resource.

T he art of leadership - where your qualities are drawing you to the forefront, making you a showpiece, is a gift from your past. It is your past saying to you: you're free;you've taken each step with care and now you're free, ahead, in the open air. When the past says to you you've things to settle, you're back in the crowds.

F resh air means solitude. Away from ego. Where there is ego in someone leading, the task to be done is held on to and what is drawn to it are the qualities that will not accomplish it perfectly. A leader needs protection from that or there is assassination. Protection from the damage he could do himself by advertising his freedom. If someone criticises, it hurts, but if someone touches, it kills and people long to catch what is free and turn it round and round and look until within seconds it becomes old.

Protection is puzzling sometimes, for it seems that around a quality that is to lead the way, a kind of crust of triviality forms that is not particularly beautiful. Where there is something invaluable, life creates a diversion. And it has to be, for as much as a leader is free, in the air that is clear of memories or influence, he has also to be buried. Not prominent as in a celebrity, but buried deep as a seed, in the earth, ugly but safe.

For ultimate leadership is not for the present, but for the future. It means to be at the outset of life, not at the conclusion; to stand tiny, vulnerable at the beginning, not public, renowned, at the end, supporting what is old. And so it is far, far more dangerous and needs protection from far more intense threats than those of assassination or overthrow. The enemy is subtle, damaging, often self-generated. In a person stretching out towards the future, a passing memory can jade the creation. It is no mass production. It is art.

And when creation has been accomplished; when quality nurtured has safely found a form in which to rest; when it is housed in the structures and systems of the future, then leadership will be to sustain it. To remember it; when life is obscuring it with busy-ness, to bring it back into expression, to keep it alive. To say yes, to remain open, when the world says no, categorically, is leadership then.

And where are you now? You are at a point of beauty, for beauty is contrast. Quality is just a seedling. It's buried, at the core and yet so strong is it, that it reaches out to meet what is oldest in life, what has really almost had it. Leadership here is to have the sharpness to see this; to see in what is old, the relics of what is invaluable, and to ease the meeting between that and what is new. It is an art, for what is young and of the future is often concealed by triviality and what is old and almost discarded, by ugliness. Yet they have to meet, for otherwise life wouldn't be a cycle. It would be a straight line.

There is a lot in leading. And most of it can be done with no one following.

THE ART OF
LEARNING
AND TEACHING

Learning and teaching are two players in the same game. When one stops, the other may keep hitting the ball, but the game is dry. There is no fun.

Learning is the ability to absorb something new into your heart and however intrusive or puzzling it may seem, to let the lesson throw into the air all that you had fixed already and know that nothing has been destroyed. For there is no such thing as learning from scratch. There is always something that has to move aside and if it will not shift, it means a philosophy has already formed and so it is too late to learn. If you want to grow fast, you have to move and stay awake, leave a bit on your plate, walk instead of being driven, say no to things that make you close your door and sit tight. Only when there is a clean mind can you start to build fixed principles for the future. Cleaning means moving.

Learning doesn't have to hurt, for where there is suppleness, an open mind, you fall softly. It used to hurt, because there was dogma. Now you have no dogma, but you have peace and peace is so accommodating.

Learning is the reward for respecting life. However trivial, recognising in it what is least obvious and yet important, like the fact that a light heart comes from thinking very deeply. And to respect and recognise, you have to slow down, look carefully and appreciate, but not stop, for lessons are in the doing, in the talking. Silence often reveals them, but carrying them into situations makes them into habits.

Learning is alone, but as in music, gains beauty when it is shared. If ten people in a room hit their own next note, the atmosphere becomes electric and in the intensity, profundities ricochet. It takes practice and a lot of pure love for each other to learn like that, for if even one is dozing, the tune drags and the sharpness is lost. But when everyone realises with equal joy that the leaps to be made inside are just as important as the business to be done with words, then nothing is ever boring and even the most menial tasks are filled with subtlety.

It is easy to learn on your own, to scrabble through irrelevance and get to the heart of things, for personal rubbish arouses no repulsion. It is just life. Harder and more strengthening is to be together again, and not mind the padding that protects the jewel. To sit together and see collectively the moment of sudden importance, even if it is not your own (which does not matter anyway because we are one in learning). To sit together and wait is a sign of love.

And love is the beginning of teaching too. For in love, there is so much patience and anonymity. There is no need to introduce yourself, for when love is in the atmosphere, but not confined to a single relationship, then everyone reaches their own potential. When love is just between two people, the one who is learning can learn as much as the teacher knows and no more. When love is very strong, personalities don't need to stun, for love itself is stunning and it illuminates the important things naturally. Where there is no love, there is ego and ego makes things important that are of interest only to some.

Love is a power that makes anyone able to do anything and forget who suggested it in the first place. And you cannot arrange love. It is just there, which is one of the things that divides the present from the future. As time goes on, teaching will just be a part of friendship. Here, now, it is separate. There are places built for learning, which is as odd as building a place for being happy in. Motivation will change too. Learning and teaching will not be because there has been a mistake or because you need to be equipped. You won't learn about children in advance of having them or about kingdoms in advance of ruling them. Learning will just be the next step forward. It will be inherent. Ideas are only isolated from things when life has broken, but trees and beauty, sky and freedom will be inseparable, so there will be no philosophy.

It takes a lot of innocence to learn about the future. And a big heart. For where there are these, there is always an exchange going on. And when this is viewed not just in terms of one birth, but of many, many, it all becomes the game it was meant to be. For whilst today I am your teacher, tomorrow I am your child. And the game is never boring, for whilst you are learning about ponds, I am on the same track further on; I am learning too, but about the sea. And when I'm the child, you are in the sea and I am playing in the puddles. And we are brought together not so much because we love each other, but because we both love water.

The water now is God.

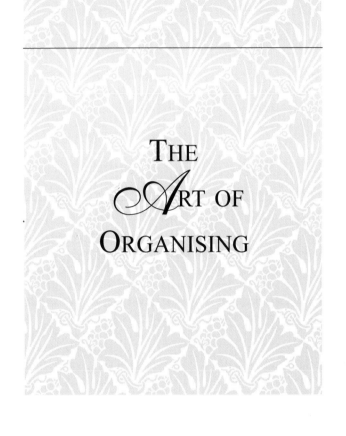

THE
ART OF
ORGANISING

There are times when this art is the foremost qualification for a task; when to be giving or sensitive is nothing more than a decoration for the doing. The doing is the thing that lets the sensitivity be expressed. Without the doing, the quality gets lost. Niceness in the air gets lost, but in a task, in the doing it is preserved. More - it multiplies.

The art of organising requires (as in contentment) the meeting of two opposites: to understand the bones of a task, but also to feel for the combination of qualities in different people, perhaps far apart, but which brought together can accomplish it.

A bad organiser does everything himself, just as a bad artist indulges only the most immediate feelings. A good organiser stretches outwards and draws in variety and richness, resources, information and makes them coherent; just as a good artist looks outwards, only using the strength of his introspection to draw things together. A great organiser can pass through physical boundaries and draw on anything, anywhere to do the task. So the enterprise grows, touches thousands, as the great artist's does also, lifting out of the physical into something indefinable, something spiritual.

To be such - your head has to be free of boundaries; so free that even the refined compartmenting done by the brain gives way to something much bigger and more fluid. Its life of checking, processing, questioning, dies to the natural innocence and optimism of the spirit. Organising is often associated with maturity. In many ways it is the art of the child whose supple brain and resilient being can even defy the fear of death. For who told him that death was bad? Who told him it was impossible to turn arms into wings? As an organiser, you need a taste for the impossible or else you are choked by red tape. You also need a big heart - for a big heart can tip the balance against officialdom, sometimes .....

Nonetheless, systems do prevail. They make themselves felt. Mastering them takes precision and knowledge. For naivety is admired only in a child. But it is still a power to retain ideals and feel their realisation intuitively. You know it will work and you will kill yourself to do it:

And there are ways to launch enormous things and stay alive. Like doing the thing in your head first. Silently, slowly, living out the accomplishment in advance; like looking at the task and however big and unwielding or however small and tedious, finding inside you, respect for it. So you want to do it. This gives power to the arm that otherwise just scratches away .....

Above all, love is needed - for love pulls everyone into sequence, pulls the right people, pulls the help. Life's emperors are the lovers. The ones in whom love is such a force, so deep, that it draws to itself what is needed and more. Much, much more. It draws the best. They are the ones for whom the task has become boneless. Others will brings the bones.

It is not superiority that turns away from the concrete and focuses on the quality. It is a matter of faith, for where the doing is relinquished, so too is any feeling about the result. But the beauty is in watching the ingredients collect and be mixed.

THE
ART OF
REFORMING

Reforming sounds harsh, enforced. Re-forming sounds like an art. The art of bringing back into form tendencies long since separated from expression. Unearthing old things, bringing them back to the surface. Inside you are capacities and powers that can move mountains. The art of reforming is bringing those back so that something new can be manifested.

It is not that you have to sit down and think of mountains or creating great civilisations, not actually calling back old structures and forms. Reforming is just bringing back into play the qualities and powers of mind that shaped visible greatness.

Force is the least conducive means of doing this. Forcing change is pushing something to the surface before it is ready. And so when it is expressed, it is only half formed. Up until now, this has been the way: to have dreams and force their realisation by making new laws, policies, pacts, but usually out of force of circumstance. Things have changed when forced, but then in periods of less pressure, it's all been gently dropped.

The art of reforming is natural. It is like when the tide turns. With a great and decisive movement, it pulls in the other direction, but naturally. Not pushed. It is the right movement. Reforming is letting yourself be turned upside down, letting things which have motivated behaviour recede, take a back seat and letting peace in; letting in things which are at the heart of you.

Reforming takes time. It is a delicate business as all art is. It has to be understood. Understanding is the energy behind force. Something major can be shifted from the 'stage' when there is understanding. It can be moved aside, leave space for a new scene. Understanding is a power and powers can either create or destroy. In this case, it is the means of dematerialising difficulty.

This is why it is useful to be quiet, because understanding is born in silence. And once silent, the mind can turn in on itself, unhampered by the noise of superficial life, turn in and bring up something ancient and invaluable. For reforming isn't just a matter of finding solutions. That is as necessary and normal as breathing. It is finding inside things that need not even fit with the present, but which are the foundation of the future.

It is a custom to think that the future is born out of the past and that they are inseparable, but if this were so, the future of your dreams would be shadowed before it even began. Silence comes in between, because silence is empty of time. Silence is silence and within a second of it, the results of thousands of years of endeavour can be held. There is nothing else that can hold the process of reformation, nothing else that is neutral and as hollow as silence is.

Still, before all reforming, there seems to be upheaval. The ground of the mind has to break, not to be destroyed, just to move. Nothing is ever destroyed. Even when continents are ripped up, thrown into the air by war. they are not destroyed, they are moving. When the mind breaks, through pressure of circumstance, there is so much sorrow. It is like a sudden last straw, a snap after a period of dullness. It is the sorrow of seeing your territory in pieces. When the mind is broken by God, there is in contrast great joy, for with every shift, a new land is forming; for every inch of the way, for every apparent landslide, there is a plan.

It begins with disentanglement. Sorrow comes when everything impacted is suddenly blown apart, like houses torn out of the ground. God works more gently, unravelling one by one, the lines of weakness in the mind, until they each stand separate, straight, seen. Then on one end, he anchors their effect, so that painlessly and with the exhilaration of understanding, you can grasp the fallacies, the mistakes, see them. Then in the lightness that this brings, like a doctor joking and injecting, he anchors to the other end their cause. Often the cause of problems is way back, seeded in the past. But always the present carries some visible equivalent, the same ingredients in a different form. With both ends 'fixed', he pulls. In the depth of silence, he brings on the storm and in one last movement, after years of intricate effort, the lines of weakness are wrenched out. Afterwards, stillness, a different stillness. Utter quiet, as the mind senses its own change.

R e-forming takes the courage of remaining awake during an operation. And yet it is easy. Just lie still .....

THE
Art of
Refreshing

What refreshes? Nature. Space untrampled, water, expanses of colour unbroken. A different angle. Looking from above, from underneath, from the future.

Caught in time and context, in a hurry, there is no chance of refreshment, unless there is a resource inside you which can wash over the immediate and bring to it something different. Not take you away, but bring something new. Children can often be refreshing, because their involvement with immediate (unless it touches them directly) is minimal. There are other more exciting things to live for. Inside. All be they snippets from things seen and heard. And because children don't try and synchronise with what is visible, their sudden words break the surface of commonplace and you laugh. Adults cannot do that or they would starve. But still, what you are inside can bring newness to a life that is repetitive. You will never stop speaking, for instance, but to speak with a mind filled with peace, makes speaking new, for where there is peace, real quietness, something new always follows.

It is the mind that is at the bottom of it all. It can make you anything: make you as an ocean, if you've thought long and hard enough about things that are profound; make you as a sky if you've let go enough to be free; make you as a stretch of land, unbuilt on, if you've relinquished sophistication. The achievement then is not so much to become natural, as a child is, cutting across routine, but to be as nature, a resource to life, not intervening, but there to go to.

For a mind to become such a gift, every second of its life has to be new. To read a book and then close it - with hands and mind. Keep it open in your mind and the impressions spill into the space which holds the future. Then you walk out of the door, into the open air, and in your mind are the closing words of what you've read. Ringing. You are neither free to appreciate what is in front of you, nor to create something new. Life is like music without a rhythm. Instead - to walk feet and mind together - this brings simplicity and strength with which to view the future.

And if there is a new world coming, it cannot be seen unless the old book has been closed. Close it and you can have a vision of what's to come. Then there is not just the simplicity of action and thought as one, but there is the beauty of action that touches the future. For even the sea is old, the land barren, the sky polluted, so they cannot, even in thought, refresh more than that which is also old: the body. See a vision of the future and two weeks of physical travelling, to find space, lightness, is yours for the cost of a second's quietness. This is refreshment so intense that it can touch another and ease their lot. A mind that is free of oldness becomes everyone's leisure, because it provides something to watch.

But where does the picture come from? Where, the vision?

In all religions, God is regarded as the 'vision giver', the one who comforts and entertains. Very much as a parent, he provides the world's children with images to play with. This is his response to their praise. But this kind of vision doesn't open the door into God's world. It is a hand extended to offer comfort or a gift, at a distance. In it there is no creativity, no participation.

Approaching God from a different angle, as a person wishing not only to be comforted but to comfort, not only to be refreshed but to refresh, the vision changes. It becomes a meeting in which the means of creating are communicated. It is information imparted with the love of someone willing to be understood.

A nd the first creation is that of a relationship with this creator. A
relationship which does spring out praise initially. Praise him for
instance as a teacher and you receive a vision, an understanding of the
future, to move towards and work for. This doesn't lull and comfort
you, but wakes up the student in you. Praise him as a father and you
receive a vision, an experience of the subtle place in which the future
is conceived. This wakes up the feeling in you and softens what,
through time, has been hurt. Praise him as the being who lifts you out
of all this flux and you get a vision of an ultimate home, still, forever
the same, for ever welcoming. And this gently folds up all the odds
and ends of oldness, classed as habits, all the pettiness of the past.

A nd when these aspects of the relationship meet and become one
in you, when all things move together and harmonise, you are
ready to enter a new age. Let someone look into your face at this point
and not be refreshed - it is impossible.

THE
ART OF
REMAINING CONTENTED
AND HAPPY

The art of remaining contented and happy rests on being a good accountant. Knowing what you've got and how to spend it. It comes from standing outside the business of it all, seeing what's left to pay off and then getting on and doing it with pleasure, because behind it there's a fortune.

Contentment is an art, for it asks for contrast: for utter rest (leaning back and watching from a position of completion) but also tireless action (to keep on moving always). It asks of you a spirit that is at once very old and very young.

Rest comes with space and space comes when there is somewhere to go and be on your own. That space is inside you. And it is as disregarded but as important as the stage on which a play is acted. For the scenes change but the stage carries it all. It is the foundation of what you do; it's behind what's said and done. And when it's strong, when it's filled with peace (and that's strong for it's peace that has lasted everything out), then it is easy to act on. It holds you up. It is restful. And then what is done reverberates and is rich, for it pays off debts and yet attracts to itself everyone's approval. It is pleasure and work combined without the consciousness of either.

That is rest. Finding space inside and operating from there. But utter rest comes from taking a break. Not in somewhere new, full of new people, new sights, but somewhere unchanged by time, of the quality of that space inside you, but multiplied a thousand times. A place into which you fit, not by assuming anything, but by shedding everything, as you cannot do with anywhere physical. It is a place free of approval or recrimination. It is not for that, for that is bound up with doing and doing isn't in its language.

Contentment is knowing that this break is always there, is not measured by what is earned or by what is directly needed. It is just there and its beauty can enter whatever you do, unlike a normal break that peters out once life resumes. This space felt, even distantly, in the background, makes life a holiday, for it fuses peace into speech, love into looking, knowledge into touching. You just have to locate it.

Still, once rested, you have to resume, to see what's owed to life and pay it. But with all the strength of peace behind you, it is the happy matter of going on 'unbrokenly', for it is that that creates the future and straightens out the past. To be contented is to do, but to stay contented is never to break the doing, never to accept a break from that.

And it is easy, for if your concern is just to get the sums right, to right the balance, and if you're careful and watch gently from the space inside, you will see what to do. You do not need to hunt for action, any more than you do for peace. It is around your neck. Ignore it and it chokes you; see it and it becomes your decoration and your wealth.

Watching your own business, you can help other people. If your eyes wander, with whatever apparent altruism, the line of fortune breaks and you are pulled down. You have to be self-centred, for then you're strong enough to lift.

There are only two places worth cherishing in life-one is in the action and the other in the space. Sometimes observing, sometimes doing and in moments, in both together. And in rarer moments still, with a mind on God who puts the whole thing in perspective and is a pleasure to be with, because he knows, and those who know as opposed to just being clever, take away complexity. Where God is concerned there is never complexity; there is always depth.

Complexity kills contentment.

There is only one thing to avoid and that is commercialism. Commercialism is doing it all for money - parading action or worse, peace. The secret in this art is that your space is all your own and that whatever you do is for yourself. However altruistic, it is for you. Once you know that, everyone can love it and breathe it in as they can a masterpiece in a public gallery. A life lived in contentment can inspire everyone and be possessed by no one but you. It is yours alone.

THE
$\mathcal{A}$RT OF
SERVING AND HELPING

It is a big thing to be a real server of people, and yet done to the utmost, it nourishes the heart of you, for in 'utterness' you are touching with your heart the seed of the matter, and so it is the heart of you that feels the return.

When the heart is used, there is a radiation outwards and what is reached is not the heads of people with the power to change things, but their hearts - and then they change themselves. Physical things follow in the wake.

You don't need any resources to serve from the heart, but you need to be rich inside. Rich means you've got space and space means an open heart. If you've got that, you can just think, and things begin to happen. But the risks are high. For whereas when you go out and meet people, mix into their lives, you can adjust and move around them; in thought, you go straight to them. A thought sent is sent. It can't be changed any more than an arrow can change its course. So there has to be no bad in the thought, not even a trace.

To serve from your heart is to give yourself to life. Not your words, or your energy or your busy-ness, but yourself. Sometimes, when the moment comes you'll not be sure and you'll take a step backwards into formality. This is called fear, as though you're losing yourself. Then you have to hold on to God, for he pulls you back to your potential. Full potential means your heart is open.

Sometimes you feel full of love, but it's stuck inside. You hold it, like a girl reluctant to become a mother. To have a good heart is one thing, but to give of it, to have it used to create something, is another. Perhaps it's because a mother knows that she'll see in the child a picture of herself.

If there was any bad in God, we'd be crippled.

So, in serving, there has to be no bad. But more. If in the space of being good, you just send a silent thought with precision, the hit of the arrow can be too hard. For silence pierces. Where there is a particular quality in the thought, like contentment, a virtue, the arrow just touches. Virtue puts its arm around a person. The change it incurs in them is therefore gentle and will last. Where there is no virtue, there is just power, the impact creates a shock and there is a spring back into the past, that's just beside you. And in the past you've helped other people but wanted them to thank you. Thanks takes you further backwards still, for it opens the account books that in real serving are closed.

When they are closed and so you're helping softly, you can look into the heart of vice even; can go back and walk someone safely home, away from their debts. That is not teaching, it is loving, being close and unafraid of what you see in them, for you can't catch anything. You're dead and can't be drawn. Vice for you is a tiger turned to paper.

Sometimes when a person has got through something, there are still the traces of the journey on their face. They're home and dry but tired. To help then is to absorb their heaviness by lifting off their means of travel: the feeling of the body. To help someone like that is to make them feel a miracle has happened, as a butterfly might feel, stepping out of its cocoon.

How do you learn to help? By being helped yourself. To have felt the impact of someone else's thought changing something inside you. To have looked into someone's face and seen not their features, but their support touching you. To have been walked home away from danger. To have been a child in spirit and felt the burden taken, the last step taken for you, leaving you accomplished and yet aware you've done nothing. When you've been served this much, you can serve. And if the words are somewhat clumsy, it doesn't matter, because the heart is seen behind them and if the wisdom seems absent, it's alright too, because it's invested in the outcome.

THE
ART OF
THINKING
AND CREATING

Thinking is the prelude to creating. It also comes before destroying, which is just as important in an age of change. It is an art, if realised as such, that requires the most effort, for it is carried by nothing visible. It is going on all the time, it determines life and yet you can't touch it, you can't see it.

Thought makes the atmosphere. When the atmosphere is right, creation can take place. Not before. When a person meditates, they begin by thinking about things that are deep and clear. This builds an atmosphere in which they can meet God. When a mind meets God, something is created.

If you want to help anyone in a way that will last, there has to be a frequent meeting with God, for out of that, something new is made. What is old will not last. Old things are made when two human minds meet and touch.

What happens in this meeting with God? Something that has been thought about is given form. Where, for instance, there have been thoughts about the passing of time and yet of life's eternity and then the mind turns with this thought, held, to God - the experience of being a traveller and yet spiritually indestructible, will become a feeling. Feelings change people, recreate them. Just thoughts do not. So the mind is changed. But more than this, the concept of the world being this double entity - passing and yet undying- becomes a reality. It happens. When you say that God creates the world, it is this you mean. That in your meeting with him, you are, with him, making things happen. If no-one held these thoughts up to his light, they would not become feelings in you and so would stay 'beyond', just as ideas. They wouldn't happen, for you are the actor, you have to know and 'do' them.

When a thought has been carried to God and brought alive, it becomes a gift for someone else. A gift means it can silence. Where it is just a thought, it will create talk.

Silence is the celebration of something having been created. It is not what you start with. If you do not actively think, but simply turn to God, empty or filled with petty concerns, nothing in his being will be attracted to you. Thought is a container for his sweetness. Where there is no thought, he won't waste his sweetness and the world needs sweetness.

Spiritual work done every day gives you containers. But they have to be strong and simple. You wouldn't pour a liqueur into a beer glass. So to get the subtlest things from God, your thoughts have to be made subtle and receptive. Then they are filled, and filled, they become gifts, medicines, saving graces.

A lot of patience is needed to carry a thought to God - without dropping it. Often things happen to it on the way. This is a pilgrimage. It is also a matter of timing. The thought is like an egg. It must be at the right time that it meets the Seed. If the thought has been analysed too much, it is broken and will not attract.

A thought given life by God can help someone. It can also call someone else to help, if a task needs doing. Ultimately you will know which thoughts to use to call people. They will be like an income proffered at a distance. People will sense a fortune coming their way.

In the future, thought will create not children of God, scientists to build, technicians to design, but children themselves. A thought taken to another person and touched will create a child. And in that thought - for there will not just be one, one 'child-creating thought' - will be folded the type of child, the gifts it will need to supplement and enrich the kingdom. Naturally. They'll be in the thought automatically, for time carries those thoughts eternally and they rise to the surface as spring does from winter.

That is a kind of marvel, even to think about. But a lot has to go for it to happen. Old ways have to pass. And thinking is bound up with old things going. So is God. A thought in the being of God makes a fire. If that fire were to spread, everything would 'go up'. It is not time for everything to go up ..   yet .. Instead there have to be 'pyres' - minds which are opened to such an extent that they can hold God's fire.

If anything goes wrong, the best thing is to build a pyre. To place brick on brick, all that has led up to something. Then light the fire. Let a spark touch the point where it all began and then watch it travel through the problem and destroy it.

Afterwards there is a mess. It has to be swept up. Sweeping up means action - doing something counteractive. Sometimes it feels as though nothing has changed. Life seems a mess still. And yet it is not. For a mess means you cannot get out, everything is stuck. But this mess is just ashes and they fly easily.

In the future death will be like this. An act of love, because it is time for the past to go. You will know your time; you will create a very strong thought. Strong thoughts make light. Meanwhile you will prepare your own body, as now you do, a pyre -very gently, with love. Not as now, will it decay, become diseased. It will be prepared, as flowers and then the light will do its task and return the body to its own form, to energy. Death will be personal, self-chosen but pre-destined and the run up will be intensely beautiful. You cannot call it destruction, for it is a matter of love. It is also just the way of the world, as it will be in a future that is now largely concealed, for its intricacies are too valuable to parade.

Thinking can be your hell, but it is also the means of making Heaven.

THE
*A*RT OF
WINNING FRIENDS

To win friendship is to win wisdom. And wisdom knows that it is all a game. It also knows that the game changes: the rules intensify, the moves complicate. There are more players, more squares. And what was just an expression of enjoyment becomes life and life is a web.

At first it is easy. You play with "things" between you, not feelings. Like children. And all your strategy is focused on that, as you pour your mind into making something. And that - the box, the house, the sandcastle - is lovely, because in it is played out the moves of your relationship, and that comes not from your emotions but from the fact that you have both discovered sand can make castles. And that is right then, because you are a child, but make a castle the basis of your friendship as an adult and it all becomes a business.

As you grow the game turns. Doing something communally is no longer the focus. Instead it is your pitted wits. The props are thrown away and you play against each other. And to keep your interest, you have to touch. "It didn't touch me" means you are disappointed. And if minds don't touch, at least bodies should. There must be intensity and at least a bit of hurt. For hurt brings the contrast. In friendship, hurt is the pattern.

The game becomes harder. The rules fluctuate. To show respect, insult is used ("because I know you can take it"); feelings are torn ("it's only the truth");possessions are exchanged ("to cement our friendship"). There are peace offerings, punishments, disappointments. And now the game is not just between two minds, but between one mind and what it thinks is the other mind. And when the other mind shows it isn't that, you are hurt, because part of you has been destroyed, the part that had the wrong idea in the first place.

Friendship needs healing. Not medicine, but healing. Medicine would make you a child again. It would say: "Do something together and let the work carry the messages for you; let the work hide the pain." It would be diversion and when you started to think more of the work than of each other, then you would think you were both better, but when the work was over, you would be naked again. Facing each other.

In the future, that will be the way to play, but you will not take from work your disguise, but you will give it your virtue.

Now friendship needs healing. So that it gets to the point where you can sit in someone's mind and be at peace - with nothing in between. And then walk out. To the point where quality is not measured by time. Where the game is a divine promiscuity, in which you may throw petals in front of someone and run and never see them in that life again, but it is as loving and beautiful as a marriage. More, because nothing is needed to cement it. It may not even be remembered. To the point where retreat and intensity and self-sacrifice just are not there. It is light and the exit is as clear as the entry.

To the point where the game can snap closed in a second and it will all be finished and you die gently. Not like now, when because your relationship has been dragged through the mud, it cannot be contracted into a second and stand identifiable like a drop of water. Dying now, whole strings of feelings dangle on. It is called attachment.

Healing is a power and it is power that is needed. For power takes you inwards to completion, so that folded in your soul are all the accomplishments that would make you a good friend. You will not perfect friendship by being a good friend now, but by contracting inwards and re-forming. Inside you there is a gift, which time has not destroyed and when that is found and brought to friendship, there will be divinity.

A very subtle love is needed to draw you inwards -and it starts with what you feel about your body. If you cannot love that first, you cannot leave the feeling of it, to be alone and think about yourself. If you haven't played the game of living in the body when it hurts, in peace, you cannot be alone. For the irritation will take you outwards again and make you fight someone. If you fight your body, you will fight other people as well and then you are in the crowd you want to be alone from.

So first you have to love and tolerate this body you live in and when you look at someone, see their soul, for looking at their body, you are looking at their battle. To tolerate means to see but not to touch and when you don't touch, things heal on their own. And when the body is healed, it too will play its part in friendship, and healthy, it will radiate a strength and subtlety that give to friendship its shine.

Inside, alone, touch God, for God's love is strong enough to take you further into who you are, which is what real love is all about. It gives you space,where involvement takes it. And as, in company, you become more and more alone and alive, you begin to learn what friendship is, for you are not the only one God is working on.

And one day, you will look out again and see an array of others who've reached their own distinction and together you'll express it. And you'll not be making a sandcastle, for that can be destroyed, but something imperishable - something for the future will be forming between you. And then you've become not each other's friend, but a friend of the earth.

THE
ART OF
WORK AND LEISURE

The Art of Work and Leisure

Work and leisure are separate, because inside there is separation. It is a time of fragments, looking at each thing isolated and strengthening it until it's time to bring all of it together and when that happens, when all things converge, completed, then everyone in your orbit will move together too. And that is the beginning of unity. And in unity, work and leisure are one, for nothing needs to be singled out and mastered -which is work, and nothing needs to be relaxed and nurtured - which is leisure, for everything is equal and has its place.

What is happening now? The strands of life are being unwound and straightened. For this, even the nastiest parts of a person are to be respected, for they are the end of the line, which traced back to its beginnings, have value. The work is to believe that someone's harshness was once their brilliance. To believe it and then to find the brilliance, for on discovering that and letting go of the rest, the future begins.

So life now is work. But its intensity is exhilarating, for you know how deeply healthy it is to clear the way back to what you were. Work is also necessary as a stopgap for the past. For in change, you are as though between two births: the past left and the standards of the future known but still at a distance. People talk of ghosts. Ghosts come between two births, when someone hasn't found a new place to be. Phantoms when you're still alive but shedding the skins are old habits. So you have to work, to be creative to change the pattern that's merged in your cells

But before all creation, there is peace and that is the leisure, which absent, means there will be oldness in the air. Peace neutralises and afterwards something new and beautiful always comes. To start your work in peace makes what you do original. And then however plain it is, it will splinter superficiality.

So it is work. But not labour, for in labour there is no peace, just tiredness. Work must be natural. And natural means knowing when the day is over and it is best just to go inside and rest. Sometimes to pull at the knots only tightens them. Instead just watch, don't touch, and know that in nature, there is a force of creativity that at times, will do the task for you. The biggest tasks finish themselves.

It takes power to stop. It is a sacrifice to sit down, but if you don't, it means you think you are the centre of the universe, when in fact there are other forces playing, besides the human one.

It is gentleness that's needed. To hear the rhythm of life and not fight. Victory is a peaceful matter. Where there are war wounds, it is defeat. To hear the rhythm means to feel the forces inside you pulling against each other - the desires against the duty, the sounds against the settled quietness - and to work with them. To hear too, the waves that shape the air outside, the waves of other minds. To work with all of that. Then you can balance things, so that when life is tipped towards leisure, it is whole-hearted and guiltless and when towards action, it is happy. When the rhythm goes unheard, you lose your logic and do what the visible tells you. You stop too early and your leisure is filled with stress or you jump towards action and trample the creation.

To work with yourself and what is around you, like this, is the beginning. But when the forces inside pull together, the desires and the duty become one, everything becomes very very quiet and you can be one of a silent army, whose impeccable discipline will usher in destruction.

Only love can do it. Law only breaks you further. Love is what brings things together, for it can run through anything and not be hurt. Peace can too, and wisdom. These are the original things in life and when they are the unbroken line through everything you do, the ground will break.

THE BRAHMA KUMARIS CENTRES
IN THE UNITED KINGDOM AND IRELAND

LONDON
Global Co-operation House, 65 Pound Lane, London. NW10 2HH
Phone; 0181 459 1400
NUNEHAM COURTENAY
Global Retreat Centre, Nuneham Park, Nuneham Courtenay,
Oxon OX44 9PG
Phone; 01865 343 551

EDINBURGH
20 Polwarth Crescent, Edinburgh, EH11 1HW
Phone; 0131 229 7220

CARDIFF
15 Morlais Street, Roath Park, Cardiff, CF2 5HQ
Phone; 01222 480 557

DUBLIN, IRELAND
36 Lansdowne Road, Ballbridge, Dublin 4, Ireland
Phone; 01353 603 967

Introductory courses in meditation are offered at each of our
centres throughout the country, free of charge.
For more information and the address of a centre near you,
please contact one of the above centres.